Old Irish Country Life
by Hugh Oram

G000272522

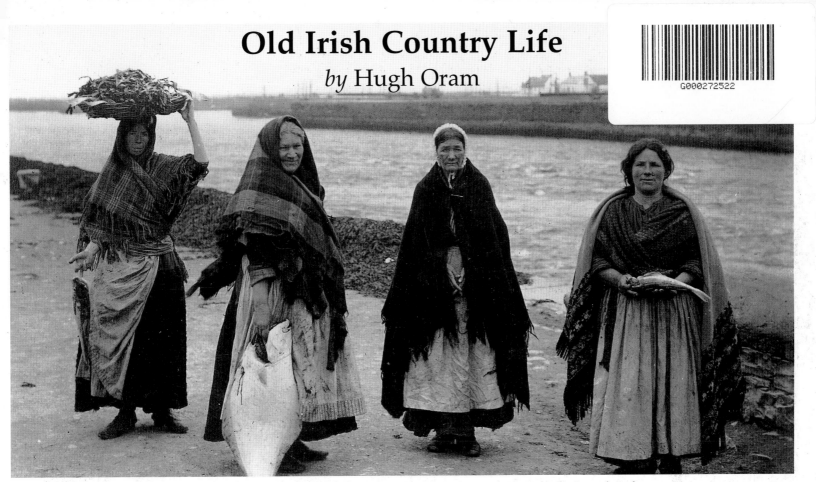

Above: Fishwives photographed on the Long Walk, by the River Corrib, returning from Galway's fish market at the Spanish Arch.

Opposite: The Claddagh, deriving its name from the old Irish for 'a stoney foreshore', was one of Ireland's oldest fishing villages and a distinctive district on the western shoreline of Galway city, developing from medieval times as the fishing village to the main town. Indeed, from time to time, the fishermen of the Claddagh elected their own 'King' the last being Martin Oliver who died in 1972. Despite its 'picturesque' thatch roofed, whitewashed, single storey cottages, Galway Corporation decided in 1934, for reasons of health and hygiene, to bulldoze the old Claddagh and replace it with modern housing. Tarred streets replaced the old cobbles, and in a stroke the old magic, tradition and antiquity of The Claddagh were destroyed. Its name survives through the traditional Claddagh finger ring, a sign of friendship, bearing a pair of hands (friendship), a heart (love) and a crown (fidelity). By tradition, if the crown is worn towards the fingers the wearer is married, and unmarried if reversed.

Text © Hugh Oram, 2007
First published in the United Kingdom, 2007,
by Stenlake Publishing Ltd.
www.stenlake.co.uk
ISBN 9781840333688

The publishers regret that they cannot supply
copies of any pictures featured in this book.

Claddagh fishermen's wives repairing nets outside their cottages, a common sight through the nineteenth and early twentieth centuries, when the sea off Galway was rich with cod, herring, mackerel, turbot, lobster and the occasional shark. When great shoals of fish appeared off the coast, the fishing boats would put out *en masse*, casting their nets in the evening, drifting overnight and bring in up to 400 mackerel each at dawn. In the nineteenth century, over 2,500 people worked Galway's inner bay, using the traditional fishing boat, the Galway Hooker, with its red sails.

Further Reading

The books listed below were used by the author during his research. None are available from Stenlake Publishing; please contact your local bookshop or reference library.

Jonathan Bell and Mervyn Watson, *Irish Farming*, 1986.
Kevin Danaher, *Ireland's Traditional Houses*, 1975.
E. Estyn Evans, *Irish Folk Ways*, 1957.
John Gallagher, *A Look Into Our Past*, 1990.
Patrick Logan, *Fair Day - The Story of Irish Fairs and Markets*, 1986.
Brid Mahon, *Land of Milk and Honey*, 1991.
Joe McGarrigle, *Donegal Past and Present*, 1995.
Frank Mitchell, *The Book of the Irish Countryside*, 1987.
Tom Neary, *The Light of Other Days: Knock Folk Museum*, 1974.
Cormac O'Gráda, *Ireland - A New Economic History, 1780-1939*, 1994.
Peadar O'Dowd, *Down by the Claddagh*, 1993.
Timothy P. O'Neill, *Life & Tradition in Rural Ireland*, 1977.
Seán Ó Súilleabháin, *Irish Folk Custom and Belief*, 1967.
Seán Ó Súilleabháin, *A Handbook of Irish Folklore*, 1970.
Mairead Reynolds, *A History of the Irish Post Office*, 1983.
David Shaw-Smith, *Irelands Traditional Crafts*, 1984.

Acknowledgements

The author wishes to thank the following: Michael Courtney, Killarney; Emer Ni Cheallaigh, Department of Irish Folklore, University College, Dublin; Séamas Mac Philib, Folklore Section, National Museum of Ireland, Castlebar, Co. Mayo; staff of the National Library of Ireland; Michael Lynch, Kerry County Archivist; Patria McWalter, Galway County Archivist; Margaret Franklin, Limerick County Library Service; Martin Walsh, Bord Iascaigh Mhara; Anna McHugh of An Post; Orla O'Toole of the Sheep and Wool Centre, Leenane, Co. Galway; Colm Sweeney, Magees, Donegal; Michael Kelly (Irish postal history); Dr Austin O'Sullivan, Irish Agricultural Museum, Johnstown Castle, Co. Wexford; Clonakilty and District Chamber of Commerce, Co. Cork; Brendan McWilliams, weather columnist, *The Irish Times*; Connie Murphy, Beara Historical Society, Castletownbere, Co. Cork; Sinead Fitzgerald of the Donkey Sanctuary at Liscarroll, Mallow, Co. Cork. Dr Jane Lyons of the geneaological website: *www.from-ireland.net*, and the website for Churchtown village, Co. Cork, *www.churchtown.net*. I would also like to pay very special tribute to my wife, Bernadette, for all her help and assistance while I was writing this book.

INTRODUCTION

The dawning of the twentieth century brought little change, or comfort, to rural Ireland. Housing, in general, remained primitive with many of the less well-off living in humble thatched cabins, often made from mud. The better-off farmhouses were well furnished, but even they were lit by candle or paraffin lamp, and cooking was done on an open fire or, perhaps, a peat burning range. Water for cooking, washing up and washing clothes came from the village pump and it was commonplace to see women carrying buckets of water on their head. The women invariably wore all-covering shawls and long skirts, following age-old tradition the idea of keeping 'in style' was unknown and it was perfectly normal for children, and some adults, to go barefoot.

Religious observances were strict and all families, from the humblest to the grandest, had their array of holy pictures and a Sacred Heart lamp, and the whole family attended Mass on Sundays - the better-off by horse and trap, the poor on foot, and often over long distances. Private transport was no more sophisticated than donkey-drawn carts, and although there was an extensive railway network, connecting all major cities and towns, few would have found a reason for such a journey.

In the absence of radio, cinema and television, people organised their own entertainment. If a farming household was particularly well off, it might have a piano and sing-songs would be arranged, especially for Sunday nights, but for most people, entertainment meant having relatives, friends and neighbours in for endless hours of chatter and story telling. The tradition of the *seanchaí* (a teller of traditional stories) was still alive in the early years of the twentieth century, and was widely popular in rural households. They still are. Ancient customs and festivals punctuated the year; St Brigid's Day on 1 February marking the start of spring (until 1752, and the change from the Julian to the Gregorian calendar, it was held on 12 February), St Patrick's Day on 17 March, the harvest-time festivals, Hallowe'en, and Christmas when every family made a big effort to ensure that the house was clean and decorated and that there was plenty of food.

Farms and homesteads grew their own vegetables, raised their own cattle, pigs and poultry, made their own butter and with home baking a strong tradition, most kitchens baked soda bread and griddle bread every day. The notion of buying factory prepared food was almost unknown, and only a few ready prepared items, such as custard powder, were available.

Just as the conditions of everyday life were harsh and basic, so too was the working life on farms. The larger ones had ploughs and steam-powered threshing machines at harvest time, but smaller farms and homesteads depended on hand tools. Vast quantities of potatoes were grown, as were cabbages and turnips, and nothing was wasted; when the wheat was harvested the straw was used for thatching. Home heating was provided by peat and much of rural social life centered around the bogs where the peat was cut using *sleáns* (turf spades). The women of the house made tea and sandwiches for the men and boys cutting the turf and, as with harvesting, turf cutting encouraged the spirit of *meitheal*, the great bonding of neighbourliness that characterized village life.

Aside from agriculture, there were few other sources of income, although as an island, fishing was a major occupation. Many of the large fishing harbours developed through the nineteenth century, included Howth in Dublin, Kilmore Quay in Co. Wexford, Dunmore East in Co. Waterford, Castletownbere in Co. Cork, Dingle in Co. Kerry, the Claddagh in Co. Galway, Greencastle in Co. Donegal, Annalong and Kilkeel in Co. Down, Clogherhead in Co. Louth, and Balbriggan and Skerries in Co. Dublin. But even the smallest inlet had one or two curraghs for fishing. The sea also provided seaweed, an important fertiliser.

In Connemara and in Co. Donegal, tweed making was a substantial home-based industry, as other work opportunities were scarce outside the cities. Dublin had its Guinness brewery, then a huge employer, and Cork also had its breweries whilst Limerick had its bacon factories. But the opportunity of large-scale manufacturing in rural areas was decades in the future. As mainland Britain came into the Industrial Revolution, Ireland could only look on, paralyzed through the lack of coal. There were, of course, small scale businesses - local tradesmen and craftsmen, including the blacksmith, the basket maker, the tailor (all clothes were hand made), the saddler, the shoemaker, and the clay pipe maker.

Many people, especially in the poverty-stricken west of Ireland, depended on money from relatives who had emigrated, usually, to the United States, to escape the endless cycle of poverty and deprivation. The pomp and vast displays of wealth and power put on by the British administration in Dublin had no relevance to everyday life in rural Ireland: the two worlds were separated by an unbridgable chasm.

Those who feature in the photographs in this book could have had no conception of how radically life and social conditions would change for their grand and great grand children. Even the advent of the Irish Free State did not herald immediate, radical change. The three main factors in changing the rural way of life were more mundane; electrification, the advent of enclosed stoves, and household running water. All are taken for granted today, but it was not until the end of the 1950s that the remoter districts could enjoy these luxuries. Thereafter, rural Ireland's old way of life vanished, and with few regrets.

An elderly housewife, or *ban a tí*, with a handful of gorse plucked from the bog for kindling, or its medicinal properties, with her patient donkey, its creels as yet unfilled, nibbling the grass. Donkeys were introduced to Ireland from Spain around 1642, and became popular for farm work and hauling turf and seaweed, by creel or cart. In 1841 the Registrar-General recorded that Ireland had 92,356 donkeys, a number set to double within 30 years. The arrival of motor transport, around 1905, reduced this number to 19,000, although they remained as working animals on some farms until the early 1970s. Today, while popular as pets, they are rarely used for work. The Donkey Sanctuary in Liscarroll, Co. Cork, looks after frail and elderly donkeys, and in mid-2005 had around 370 in its care, most, previously kept as pets.

A woman in a black woollen shawl, photographed around 1900, and her donkey with its straw topped creels, probably, filled with potatoes. The shawl, in widespread use across Ireland until the 1950s, except on travelling women, was a variant of the traditional full length cloak. It had fallen out of fashion in the 1840s but its regional variations had included the black Kinsale Cloak, dating from medieval times, which covered only the head and shoulders, and the blue, full length, Waterford Cloak, with its detachable hood.

Right: Plucking fowl for market was a year round task, usually carried out by the young women on the larger farms, whilst geese and turkeys were reared, mainly, for the Christmas market. The exotic guinea fowl was the preserve of better-off farms where, also, the medieval tradition of keeping pigeons was maintained. On smallholdings, a few hens and ducks provided eggs for the house and, if reasonably well off, a couple of geese or a turkey or two, for the family Christmas.

This photograph of a driver on his donkey cart outside Donoghue's pub-cum-grocery shop in Killarney's Fair Hill was taken by Louis Anthony, a French–born photographer, who had a studio in Killarney's High Street from 1890 until 1920. The driver cannot be named but standing, just visible, in the doorway is the proprietor, Julia Donoghue who occupied the premises from the early 1890s until at least 1905.

A little Bit of Ireland.

This well dressed woman was perhaps the wife of the gentleman farmer, who owned the farm steading in the background. The cottages appear well maintained and neatly thatched, and probably stood in the rich dairy-farming country of the Golden Vale, that runs through counties Limerick and Tipperary. The thatching style also suggests this area, being close enough to the windy west coast to be well tied down with, clearly visible, ropes.

7

Two small children on a cart that would have been used for transporting farm produce to the local weekly market. In the eighteenth century a wheeled cart of any kind was a great novelty, but by the early 1800s the Scotch cart, its large wheels coping well with the poor roads, was popular in the northern part of Ireland, before spreading throughout the whole island.

A farmer at his steading, loading that day's milk for delivery to the local creamery, or collection point at a nearby crossroads. Typical of the hundreds of creameries up and down the country was the Churchtown Dairy Factory in Co. Cork, a co-operative owned by local farmers, with a daily intake of about 3,000 gallons (13,500 litres). The development of co-operative creameries began in the late 1880s; the first opening at Drumcollogher, Co Limerick, in 1889, shortly before Churchtown, which closed in 1982. The movement spread fast, and by 1905 there were 275 co-op creameries across Ireland. During the War of Independence (1919-1921), British military forces burned down many creameries, considering them centres of rebellion against the Crown. From the 1940s, local creameries began to lose their importance, and by 1995, only 36 were left. Today, a handful of companies - including Glanbia, Kerry Foods and Lakeland Dairies, control the milk processing business. His delivery made, the farmer in the photograph may have come home with his can full of 'skim' - the left over from the cream and butter making process, to fatten his pigs or calves.

A Connemara woman and her faithful sheepdog bringing home the turf, a common sight on the back roads of rural Ireland until the 1950s. Designed to straddle the donkey's back, the woven basketwork creels came in a number of distinct regional patterns, but were usually fashioned from sally rods (willow twigs). As the seasons revolved, they could be loaded with turf, as in the photograph, seaweed (widely used as a fertiliser), or potatoes.

The contents of a cart, hauled by a weary donkey, are being discussed by a travelling salesman and a customer outside Pettigrew's butter and grain store in a small, unidentified, town in Co Waterford. Pettigrew is a Scottish name, but branches of the family are well established in Ireland - one branch having settled at Aughnacloy, Co Tyrone, in the 18th century. The posters on the gates to the left suggest Co. Waterford - Robertson, Ledlie & Ferguson, had large drapery stores in Belfast, Dublin, Cork and Waterford, but this poster advertises the latest fashions in its Waterford store. The other poster advertises a railway excursion to Dublin. To the right is a pub, closed for the day, whilst in the channel in front a cat is dozing.

A typical market day in the West of Ireland, the women wearing their traditional shawls, while the one on the right has a large basket woven from willow and used for carrying eggs. In contrast, the small case with handle, on the ground beside the woman on the left, would be fashionable today! A jumble of donkeys and carts make up the middle distance, while in the background stacks of timber for firewood lie under tarpaulins.

Until the early 1900s, primitive houses, especially in remoter parts, had no facilities of any kind, and pigs were an integral part of the family home. They were often the means of paying the rent, and kept outside, in the mud, until the weather turned bad, especially in winter, when they were brought inside, giving rise to the old expression "pigs in the parlour". All classes of labourers kept at least one pig, even the better off cottiers, who worked for their farm employer all the year round, renting their cabin and 0.2 ha (half an acre) of potato garden for around 30 shillings a year. They might also have kept a calf or two.

Judging by the exuberance of some of the women in this photograph, people from better off families are enjoying a wedding party, on a mountain road somewhere in the west of Ireland. Some of the women are wearing the fashions of the time, blouses and long skirts, while others, including teenagers, wear the much more traditional all-enveloping woollen shawl. The young boys at the front of the photograph are in their Sunday best, while one young girl, at the far left, wears a fashionable boater.

Horses and carts on the steep street of an unnamed town although the slated, rather than thatched, roofing suggests it is in Ulster - for the weekly market. It would not be surprising to find that the farmers had travelled as far as 40 km that morning. The adults are reasonably well dressed, but many of the younger children are barefoot and, rather unusually, the granite slabbed pavements are clean, whilst the untarred roadway is a morass of mud.

Killing the pig was an important rural ceremony and social occasion with neighbours lending a hand. Afterwards, they would enjoy tea and home made bread and cakes, and sometimes a whiskey or two. It was a time to exchange neighbourhood news, and local gossip got a great airing. Superstition also attended, a pig never being killed during a month containing the letter 'R', and if the killing was done during a full moon, the meat, it was believed, increased in size. The whole animal was used; the head being boiled to a jelly, and flavoured with pepper, spices and nutmeg, and the blood used for black puddings, or *drisheen* in the Cork area. The women cured the ham and bacon, using salt, saltpetre and brown sugar, and for the smoking, some houses had hangers in the ceiling. The earliest bacon factory, Mattersons, started in Limerick in 1816, and James O'Mara, who cured bacon in the basement of his house in Toomevara, Co Tipperary, set up a bacon factory in Roches Street, Limerick in 1839. Limerick's tradition of bacon factories lasted almost exactly a century.

This humble, rough stone, peasants cabin with its rudimentary thatched roof, lashed down against the winds by ropes, was typical of the west of Ireland. The *Bothán Scóir*, labourer's cottage, was better built, but again, had one room, with a packed earth floor, for cooking, eating, and sleeping. The man's ragged trousers also indicate extreme poverty. The 1841 Census shows Ireland had a population of 8,175,124, with nearly half the rural population living in mud cabins, so perhaps this couple was lucky that theirs was of stone. In 2006 the island of Ireland had a population of 5.8 million, with 4.2 million in the Republic and the remainder in the province of Northern Ireland.

An Irish Cabin.

A family of children outside their cabin, around 1903, with their fattened pig and goats. The number of animals kept depended, of course, on the size of the farm or holding, and the prosperity of the family, but even the fairly poor would hope to keep one cow, for milk, and perhaps one or two pigs for bacon and ham. Goats also produced milk - and kept the grass down.

A modest farmyard, with pigs and geese, and the woman of the house, babe in arms, seeing her husband off to the creamery with the churn of milk, produced, perhaps, by their two cows.

An elderly woman outside her home near Glengarriff (*An Gleann Garbh*, the rugged glen) in west Co. Cork near the Co. Kerry border. Both the house and her mode of dress were typical of this area in the late nineteenth century, but who was she? Tantalizingly, the photograph from which this image comes is inscribed 'Glengariff, Ireland, Sunday May 23rd 1897' – but does not name her. Although renowned for its oak woodland, which has survived, the village had a history of deprivation and poverty, and suffered more than most during the Great Famine. Lady Henrietta Chatterton (1806-1876), wife of Sir William Abraham Chatterton of Castle Mahon, Co. Cork, visited Glengarriff in 1838 as part of her rambles through the south of Ireland, and published her observations in book form *'Rambles in the South of Ireland'* on its extreme poverty, broken down cottages, subsistence farming and meagre fishing. The opening of the West Cork Railway to Bantry in July 1881 brought 'aristocratic tourism', with holidaymakers arriving in Bantry and taking the 'Prince of Wales' route to Killarney, overnighting in the Eccles Hotel (opened 1740 and still going strong) at Glengarriff and on to Kenmare. Only in the twentieth century did the living conditions for poor people around Glengarriff improve.

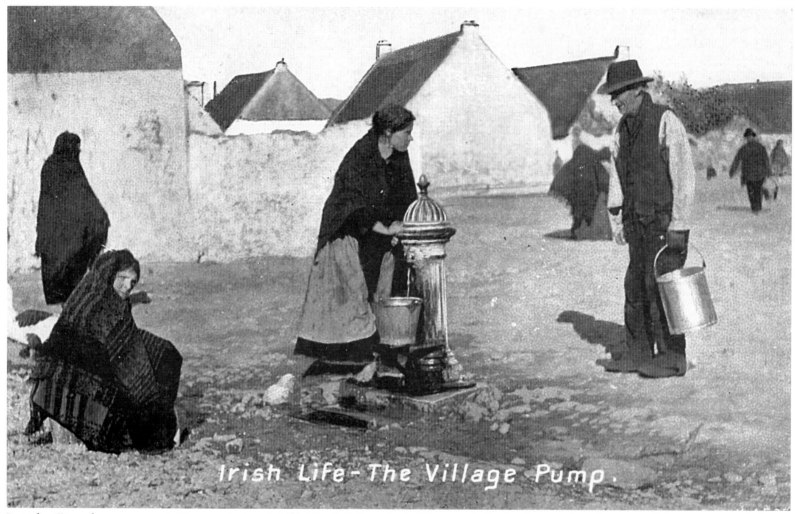

Irish Life - The Village Pump.

In each village, the pump - probably manufactured at the Glenfield Foundry in Kilmarnock, Scotland – was the sole source of clean water, until phased out in the 1930s with the spread of domestic supplies. A few survived until the 1970s, but, with the possible exception of the 'Wheel of Fortune' pump – from the resemblance of its operating wheel to the wheel depicted on tarot cards – in Clonakilty, Co. Cork, and dating from around 1848, those left today remain as ornaments.

Irish Life.—A Typical Village Scene.

A typical, late nineteenth century, village street scene. On the right, surrounded by a stone base, is a store of firewood, with washing drying on top. The two women are in conventional dress; the older women, on the left, wearing a black cloak and bonnet, whilst her younger companion has a looser, more modern, woollen shawl. The man in the distance, by the appearance of his cap, was a postman. All the cottages are thatch roofed - slated roofs were rare in those days - and the roadway is compressed earth with a primitive cobbled pavement beside the cottages. In the twentieth century, village housing throughout Ireland was upgraded and the roads surfaced with tarmacadam.

This photograph, captioned 'Irish peasantry', spans the generations, although life expectancy for rural people was not good, even in the late nineteenth century, so rudimentary was health care. The towns and cities had their hospitals and smaller communities their dispensaries, but there were no 'family doctors' in rural areas, hence the high dependence on natural treatments and herbal remedies. Bone setting, following a fracture, was performed by a local with the 'gift' - but no formal medical training. Exacerbated by poverty, malnutrition and contaminated water; dysentery, cholera (Dublin had epidemics in 1831-32 and 1849), tuberculosis, malaria, and even yellow fever, were endemic across Ireland into the latter half of the nineteenth century, and few rural men lived beyond 50 years. As late as 1946 the average life expectancy in the country as a whole was 60 for men and 62 for women. The current respective figures are 75 and 80.

Evicted tenant & his family

A typical post-famine eviction scene, witnessed regularly in rural areas from the mid-1850s. Albeit the worst of the famine had passed, it was common to see families, like this one, camped out in the ruins of their house. Between 1849 and 1854, between 250,000 and 500,000, mainly rural, people were forced from their homes or smallholdings, usually for rent arrears, and in the fifty years to the end of the nineteenth century evictions became so common that their numbers were not accurately recorded. Landlords were attracted to the better returns from large-scale sheep farms. The fortunate emigrated to America and the less fortunate to the workhouse. An amendment to the 1838 Irish Poor Law Act, the Gregory Clause (after its initiator, the Dublin MP, William Gregory), was enacted in 1847 whereby anyone holding less than one quarter of an acre of land was eligible for public assistance - the workhouse. Often they survived on little more than turnip tops. In one case on Achill Island, Co. Mayo, in 1850 an old man who lived in a house occupied by his forefathers, was forced out, carrying his bedridden wife in his arms. The Land Act of 1870 was the first in a series passed in 1881, 1885, 1887 and 1891. The most significant, allowing tenants to buy their land, came in 1903, and between then and 1920 some nine million acres (3,642,300 ha) of land were sold off.

IRISH LIFE. AN EVICTION, KILLARNEY.

Captioned, 'An Eviction', this early twentieth century photograph of Killarney's Glebe Lane, or to give it its proper name, Boherkaele Lane, which still exists - is more simply, a picture of everyday life in one of Killarney's famed lanes. The area around High Street and New Street has some 20 other lanes, including Old Market Lane, once the heart of Killarney's commercial quarter, and Back Lane today so colourful after its renovation, but once the most densely populated lane complex in Killarney. In the nineteenth century, they held a mixture of homes and businesses, which, during the twentieth century, became run-down and unfashionable, until vast renovation programmes in the 1980s. The barrels on the right are suggestive of a cooperage, and both the 1901 and 1911 Census Returns show the cooper, Maurice O'Malley, Senior and his son, also, Maurice, as residing in the Lane.

A primitive form of spinning wheel with, unusually, a man holding the threads. By the end of the seventeenth century, the Irish woollen industry was so strong that in 1699 the British parliament, to protect mainland manufacturers, restricted its export. This crippled the trade, but the situation was saved by the start of the linen industry and the Linen Board set up to promote it. It gave spinning wheels to the poor, encouraging them to develop a livelihood. Another distribution of spinning wheels came at the end of the eighteenth century, to encourage the growth of flax, particularly in the nine counties of Ulster. An index of the recipient's names runs to 52,641, living in every county except two, Dublin and Wicklow. The tweed industry also began to develop, in regions like Co. Donegal, and there was further demand for spinning wheels.

A woman spinning wool for tweed outside her home in west Co. Donegal where the old craft was centred around Ardara. These women had to work hard, for a loom in the hands of a skilled weaver could produce 90 feet of (two feet wide) tweed per day. They took their patterns from nature, 'herringbone' from their fish, and 'salt and pepper' from the quartz of their mountains. There were thriving tweed markets at Ardara, Kilcar and Glencolumkille in Donegal and the county's first tweed factory, McNutts at Downings in north Donegal, started production in 1890. Today, like its cousin in the Scottish borders, the industry has declined, leaving only some 30 home weavers still practising the craft.

This photograph, and the following five, forms part of a series of 12 photographs by the Dublin based photographer William Lawrence (1840-1932) of Sackville Street (now O'Connell Street), entitled, 'The Connemara Peasant Home-Spun Industry' and depicts the processing of wool, from sheep to finished product. The images cannot be dated, but were commissioned by Robert McKeown, proprietor of the Leenane Hotel near Clifden in west Co. Galway. This first one shows wool being dried on rope lines on rising ground above the hotel, with its weaving workshop towards the right, and the inlet of Killary Harbour, Irelands only fjord, beyond. Wool was usually draped over stone walls to dry, but the quantity used here demanded extra space. The locally produced wool came from the native *Cladóir* breed, whose wool was very fine, and the Galway/Roscommon breed, which produced good quality wool, and imported Mountain Blackface, whose wool was long and coarse.

Women teasing the wool after drying – separating or fluffing up the fibres and picking out any foreign matter not removed by the washing. This light work could be done by children, usually indoors, although for this 'staged' photograph Lawrence has brought them outside, to overcome the then contemporary limitations of interior photography.

To prepare it for spinning, the wool was carded using wooden paddles with angled wire tines, rather like a dog or cat brush, the teased wool being spread across one paddle and combed out with the other.

The spinning wheel being used here was known as the Big Wheel or the Walking Wheel, which first appeared in Middle Ages Europe but had became indigenous to Connemara and Co. Kerry. After spinning a yard or so of thread, the spinner walks back to the wheel, winding the yarn onto a spindle and repeating the process, over and over, until the spindle was loaded.

Local weaver, Tom Kerrigan in the workshop at the Leenane Hotel. During the 1890s the Congested Districts Board introduced the automatic fly shuttle loom (invented by John Kay in 1733 – the board prided itself in being abreast of technology!), manufactured in mainland Britain, that dispensed with the hand thrown process and sped up production. Cottage weavers gradually disappeared from Connemara, being replaced by factory production in the 1930s, which in turn died out in the 1970s.

Once woven, the tweed was given a final wash in the river, by bare-footed men, before going for sale.

The Turf Harvest.

Turf harvesting in western Connemara, where the roughly hewn lumps of turf in the foreground, having been cut using one of many regional variations of the *sleán* or turf spade, have yet to be gathered into the stacks, as seen beyond.

Turf was cut in spring and early summer and stacked, as seen in this photograph, at the cutting site to dry out. Turf cutting and stacking was carried out across Ireland (a mid-nineteenth century survey found about 1.15 million hectares was bogland), but with over 60% of West Co. Donegal comprising of bogland, almost everyone in the county was an expert.

A young boy leads a turf laden donkey from a bog on which his family would have had communal rights. And, although he has been photographed alone, turf cutting would have involved the whole family – the women taking tea and bread to the men cutting the following winter's fuel.

A woman and her donkey, with its peat loaded panniers, pictured on a comparatively well-made road somewhere in Co. Galway or Co. Mayo. The telegraph poles are a reminder of the early introduction of telegraphy in Ireland – the first trans-Atlantic cable being laid between Newfoundland and Co. Kerry in 1866 and how its popularity quickly grew. In 1870 all the electric telegraph companies in Great Britain and Ireland were brought under the control of the General Post Office.

Washing Day in Ireland.

The business of washing clothes was, of course, done entirely by hand – sometimes with warm water and soap, but sometimes, in the river, with some towns and villages such as Sixmilebridge in Co. Clare, having specially designated riverside ledges. In this 1895 photograph, the woman is using a scrubbing board in a tub of warm water, whilst one of her children tends the fire heating the rinse, and the donkey waits patiently with the next cartful of firewood.

Left: A west coast fisherman and his fishing coracle, with its hide covered wooden frame, which was sturdy enough to endure the often stormy Atlantic conditions in which he worked. The more sophisticated curraghs (or, more properly currachs) of which there were some 16 regional variations, another of which is shown below, had canvas, rather than hide, covered hulls, with the smallest being six feet (two metres) in length. Due to the lack of conventional harbours they became popular along the coast and in the early 1900s, there were 500 on the Co. Clare coast alone, giving employment to 1,000 fishermen. Until the late 1950s, fishermen on Achill Island, Co. Mayo, still used curraghs to hunt basking sharks, so valuable was their oil as a fine-grade aircraft lubricant. Today, curraghs are used mainly for racing, the annual turf sailing festival in Kinvara, south Galway, commemorating the crossing of Galway Bay from Connemara with loads of turf, and the salmon fishing along the River Shannon.

Below: Currachs were also popular on the River Boyne area in eastern Ireland. They varied in size, from the six feet (two metres) coracle (the origin of the word currach) to the 26 feet (eight metres) *naomhog*, which was popular off the west Kerry coast and which represented the high point in the evolution of currach design. In 2002, the National Museum of Ireland's Country Life Section at Castlebar, Co Mayo, built a replica of the traditional Belderrig (Co Mayo) currach, which was in use off the north Mayo coast until the 1950s.

The fish market in Galway stood across the River Corrib from The Claddagh, where Galway's fishermen lived. The old fish market had been at the east end of the bridge across the river, but was such a public nuisance, that in 1800 the military governor, General Meyrick, opened a subscription fund for the building of a new market close to the Spanish Arch. It included several sheds, a pump and a porter's lodge and was such an improvement on the old market, that it was said to be the best in the kingdom.

A 1905 view of the old Galway fish market, the ruins of the Spanish Arch more visible, with the fishwives, gathering together their empty fish barrels, having sold all their wares. The eighteenth century Spanish Arch still exists, but due to developments over the past 20 years, the area is scarcely recognisable from this photograph.

Above: Seaweed harvesting was an industry along the coastal counties of Donegal, Mayo, Galway and Kerry, where it was gathered at low tide, tied into anchored bundles and collected on the rising tide by curraghs. As in this photograph, it was also harvested by women, using short bladed knives. Originally used as fertiliser, it was later processed for iodine, glass, animal feeds and food additives. Today's (2006) annual harvest of 45,000 tonnes is a fraction of that once gathered.

Opposite: Seaweed being loaded on to a donkey cart at low tide. It is not known where this inlet is, but judging by the beached boats, the men were also fishermen.

Loading Seaweed.

This 1959 photograph shows granite kerbstones being fashioned at Annalong, on the east coast of Co. Down, under the shadow of the Mountains of Mourne. The quarrying and shipping of Mourne Granite from the small fishing village of Annalong in the eighteenth century, was further developed in 1824 with a new quarry, and funicular railway, in nearby Newcastle. The demand for kerbstones increased dramatically with the development of towns and cities in both Ireland and mainland Britain - some 60% of Liverpool's kerbstones came from the Mournes, and many miles of the highways and byways of London, Manchester and Birmingham have verges lined with blocks cut from these mountains. The special techniques and stone-working skills flourished until the introduction of pre-cast concrete in the early twentieth century, but as quarries closed, many of the artisans emigrated to Canada and the United States, where their skills, particularly on the eastern seaboard, were much sought.

Turnip harvesting was arduous, repetitive and back breaking work worsened in bad weather by muddy conditions. Pulling the root from the ground, the turnip was topped and tailed with a sickle shaped knife, a snagger. Manual turnip harvesting continued in parts of Ireland until the 1970s, before mechanical harvesting was widespread.

Digging potatoes in the Mangerton area of Killarney, Co. Kerry, where the most popular varieties were Kerr's Pink and Golden Wonder. In the mid-nineteenth century, after the famine, the average Irish household consumed 14 lbs of potatoes a day; a labouring man being considered well off if he had a noggin, a wooden, quarter pint drinking cup, of buttermilk with his meal. In 1897 Co. Kerry had 25,000 acres (10,000 hectares) planted in potato, mostly in smallholdings, and nationally the figure was 500,000 acres (200,000 hectares), about 80% of which was the variety Champion introduced in 1876. Today, potatoes are grown on less than 30,000 acres (12,000 hectares) and of the 650 farmers growing them, half the crop is grown on 50 farms.

'An Irish Milkmaid' milking a white Shorthorn cow, probably on her family's smallholding - milkmaids being employed on the larger farms. St. Brigid, born in Leinster about AD 455, was their patron saint through her founding the abbey in Kildare town, which had a herd of cows. The milkmaids' practice of making the sign of the cross on a nearby surface, after dipping their finger in the milk froth, dates from that time. The spread of rural electrification in the 1950s brought mechanization, and by the early 1970s hand milking had vanished, the machinery becoming the preserve of the menfolk.

Pig fairs were once commonplace in market towns, especially in Co. Cavan and Co. Monaghan, where pig farming is still important. One of the best fairs was at Bailieborough, Co. Cavan where, under a charter granted in 1702, a pig fair was held on the Old Green on first Monday of each month. Between 1603 and 1625, rights were granted for no less than 325 fairs in Ireland, the oldest being the twelfth century, annual horse fair in Muff, near Virginia, Co. Cavan.

An early twentieth century market day in Kilronan, the 'capital' of Inishmore, the largest of the three Aran Islands, off the west coast. The 1891 Census shows the Aran Islands had a population of 2,907, that Inishmore had 397 houses, and that Irish was spoken regularly by 88% of the population, whilst 77% of adults spoke no English. On the very small farms of Inishmore, with their stone wall divided fields, farmers grew potatoes and kept cows for milk. With everything else coming from the mainland, including turf from Connemara, the weekly market by the harbour was an important event. The barrels in the photograph were used for salted mackerel, again, brought from the mainland, rather than caught locally.

Livestock fairs were widespread in Ireland until the 1950s, but the great October Fair in Ballinasloe, Co. Galway, still held today, was particularly noted for its sheep sales; in 1853, 100,000 sheep came under the auctioneer's hammer. Other, lesser, sheep fairs were at Birr in Co. Offaly, (annually, on St Brigid's Day, 1st February) until the early 1800s, and at Bawn in Kilkenny each May and September. Wool markets were also popular, the greatest, in the nineteenth century, being, again, at Ballinasloe every July, with others at Dublin, Waterford, Mountrath in Co. Laois and Maryborough (now Portlaoise). In the nineteenth century, the Co. Wexford village of Taghmon held 28 fairs a year – two in each month with a special one for Christmas. They held their last one in 1961. Until the early twentieth century, fairs were not just for selling and buying livestock and poultry – rural craftsmen – basket makers, coopers, nail makers and tinsmiths – also sold their wares, and farming families sold butter, eggs and knitwear.

IRISH LIFE SHEEP AND CATTLE FAIR 4338

Roadside Butter Market.

Any farm or homestead making their own butter, and being close to a town or a main thoroughfare, would sell it at the roadside. This particular operation seems sophisticated for its time, with baskets for the butter and weighing scales.

Irish Life:
"Granny," the Fruit Seller.

This bare-footed, 'Granny' the Fruit Seller, and her ilk, were a common sight in towns and villages the length and breadth of Ireland in the late nineteenth century, displaying a variety of fruits, some native apples and pears, and oranges, then considered exotic, imported through Dublin or Cork, and bought from itinerant wholesalers.

The well-maintained exterior appearance of this farmhouse suggests it was home to a better-off family, perhaps, once again, in Munster's prosperous Golden Vale milk-producing area. Here, a typical family would own 100 acres (40 hectares) of land with vegetable garden and orchard - and 20 cows. Today, the many different styles of late nineteenth and early twentieth-century farmhouses, especially those built in Munster, can be seen restored at Bunratty Folk Park, Co. Clare.

Most nineteenth century rural houses had thatched roofs, the owners relying on travelling thatchers to repair or replace them. The thatching material varied, but included reeds from rivers and lakes, and wheat, oat and rye straw. Wheat was most commonly used for roofs up to eight inches (20 cms) thick. Roofing styles also varied. Along the windy western seaboard the thatch was roped down, whilst in the midlands, where winds are much less severe, sally rods (willow branches) were used to keep the thatch in place. The thatched cottage, so characteristic of the Irish countryside, can still be found on the west coast from Donegal to Kerry, and in the east at Skerries, north of Dublin, once renowned for its numbers of thatched houses. Today only half a dozen remain. By 1989 just nineteen thatched cottages remained on the Aran Islands, and by 1993 there were only 150 in the whole of Northern Ireland.

An elderly couple, from the West of Ireland, judging by the stone walls typical of County Galway, around 1903. Both are wearing rough and ready, but sturdy, boots, although the woman is not typically dressed for the era, not having a shawl, merely a scarf covering her head. Both have the blackthorn sticks, widely used by people then when out walking, to clear brambles on the path. Their very basic cottage would have been without running water, and the one room, with its primitive open fire, would have served as kitchen, living room and bedroom. Their diet would have been of potatoes and turnip, with the luxury of ham or cured bacon from time to time.

It cannot be said with certainty where D Connery's pub was, but this late nineteenth - early twentieth century man, with his top hat, waistcoat, broad tie and clay pipe is typical of the period. The location may have been in Co. Wexford, where the name Connery was common. The Scottish actor, Sir Sean Connery's family were from this area, his great grandfather having been a traveller here before migrating to Scotland, where he died in Glasgow in 1914.